Frank Lloyd Wright

Doraine Bennett

rourkeeducationalmedia.com

D1533729

Teacher Notes available at
rem4teachers.com

www.rourkeeducationalmedia.com

PHOTO CREDITS: cover, title page, pages 5, 12, 13, 20, 22; page 6a: © red_frog; page 6b: © courtesy Aldebaran Farm ; page 7, 17, 19: © Wikipedia; page 8: © George Pudlo; page 10: © Wikipedia/Dave Pape; page 14: © Surfsupusa; page 15: © Library of Congress; page 16: © Buffalo History Museum; page 18a: © Henryic Sadura; page 18b: © Benkrut; page 21: © Sean Pavone

Edited by: Precious McKenzie

Cover and interior design by: Renee Brady

Library of Congress PCN Data

Frank Lloyd Wright / Doraine Bennett (Little World Biographies)
ISBN 978-1-61810-157-0 (hard cover)(alk. paper)
ISBN 978-1-61810-290-4 (soft cover)
ISBN 978-1-61810-413-7 (e-Book)
Library of Congress Control Number: 2011945882

Rourke Educational Media
Printed in the United States of America,
North Mankato, Minnesota

Educational Media

rourkeeducationalmedia.com
customerservice@rourkeeducationalmedia.com • PO Box 643328 Vero Beach, Florida 32964

Table of Contents

An Early Dream

Have you ever dreamed of designing beautiful buildings? From the time he was young, Frank Lloyd Wright wanted to be an **architect**.

Frank Lloyd Wright became one of America's best architects.

Spring Green, Wisconsin

Frank's uncle had a farm in Wisconsin. Spending summers on the farm would later influence Frank's designs.

In the 1890s Chicago was a booming town which helped Frank launch his career.

Frank moved to Chicago in 1887. He would soon work for the architectural firm of Adler and Sullivan. Robert Sullivan helped Frank learn how to design structures.

George Blossom Home, 1892.

As a young architect, Frank wanted to design buildings that reminded him of nature. He believed the **function** of a building should determine its shape.

Robert G. Emmond Home, 1892.

W. Irving Clark Home, 1893.

Designing Homes

Frank drew plans for a new kind of house. It was long and low like the wide American **prairie**. Inside it had big, open rooms.

The Prairie House, built in 1901, still stands today.

Frank built with materials from nature. He used stones and wood he could find nearby.

Frank moved back to Wisconsin and built a unique house for himself. He called it Taliesin.

Taliesin looked unlike any other American home at that time. Over the years, Frank changed and rebuilt Taliesin.

Then a friend asked Frank to plan a house for him. He would build the house over a waterfall. He called it Falling Water.

Falling Water is his most famous house. It looks like it is floating over the waterfall. People from all over the world come to see it.

Designing Public Buildings

The Larkin Building was built in 1904 in Buffalo, New York.

Frank designed The Larkin Building. It had skylights in the roof, a restaurant on the top floor, and an outside deck. Frank added an indoor garden and a library.

The Imperial Hotel in Japan.

Frank went to Japan to build a hotel. Later, there was an **earthquake**. The ground shook and buildings everywhere fell. But not Frank's hotel. It stood strong.

Frank designed the Annunciation Greek Orthodox Church in Milwaukee, Wisconsin. Its shape is a circle.

Frank designed the Unitarian Church in Sherwood Hills, Wisconsin. Its shape is a triangle.

Frank built many churches.

Florida Southern College is the world's largest collection of Frank Lloyd Wright buildings on one site.

He built a community center in Marin County, California, and a college in Florida. Frank wanted the buildings to be beautiful like the land.

Fast Facts

Frank started a school for architects at Taliesin. Men and women came to learn from him.

Frank's last building was the Guggenheim Museum in New York City. Most people think it is his best work. He was an **innovative** architect who wasn't afraid to try new things!

Timeline

1867	Frank born June 8 in Richland Center, Wisconsin
1887	Moved to Chicago
1901	Designed Prairie House
1911	Built Taliesin
1915	Started Imperial Hotel in Japan
1932	Started the school at Taliesin
1935	Built Falling Water
1943	Began work on the Guggenheim Museum
1959	Frank died

Glossary

architect (AR-ki-tekt): a person who draws plans for a building

earthquake (URTH-kwayk): shaking in part of the Earth's surface

function (FUHNGK-shuhn): the purpose or role

innovative (in-uh-VAY-tiv): to do something in a new way

prairie (PRAIR-ee): land that is mostly flat and grassy

Index

Websites

www.pbs.org/flw/buildings/
www.franklloydwright.org
www.oprf.com/flw/

About the Author

Doraine Bennett lives in Georgia with her husband. She creates books on CDs for her grandchildren in Texas and Nigeria. She enjoys growing flowers, catching tadpoles in the creek behind her house, and writing books for children.

Ask The Author!
www.rem4students.com